OUR CIRCLE,

A collection of Indigenous and non-Indigenous students wanted to share a series of stories based on the seven sacred teachings: Humility, Love, Courage, Honestly, Truth, Wisdom, and Respect.

This is "Our Circle" in which we chose to share our stories, but we hoped that everyone could say that this is "My Story".

Humility: The story of one Indigenous youth who dreams and aspires to find his future by attending high school in the city. While the choice to move was difficult for his family there is more opportunity in the city. The youth soon realizes that the transition is hard and confusing, for the Indigenous student is alone. Soon, he will become lost in a system which was not created to support his people.

It has been researched that up to 45% of Indigenous students will fail to graduate with a high school diploma. As a nation, we must acknowledge that we are failing our future generations. Before change can happen there needs to be an understanding of the problem. This is the story of Nekosis.

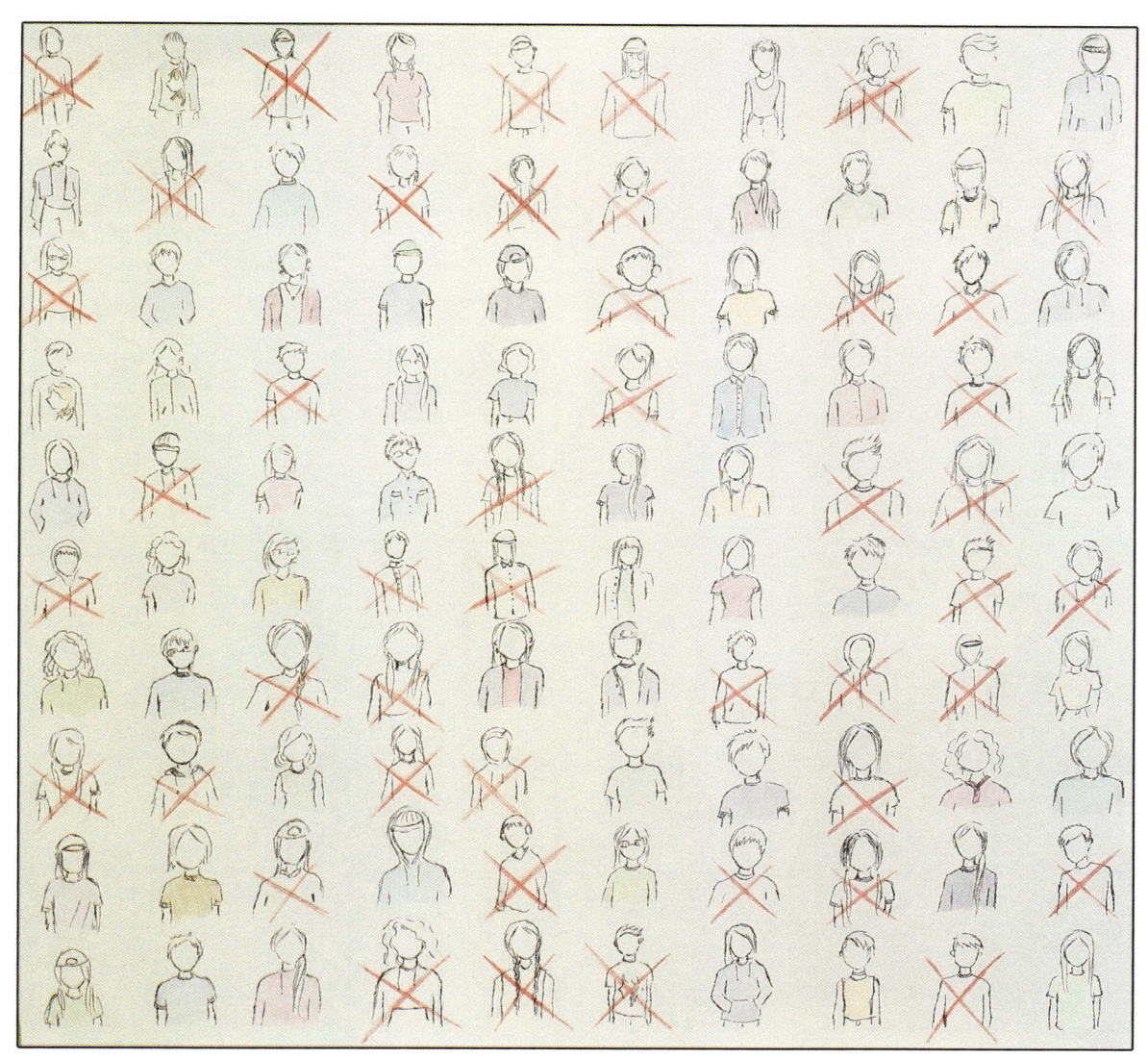

THIS DRAWING REPRESENTS ONE HUNDRED INDIGENOUS STUDENTS, AND THE FORTY-FIVE INDIGENOUS STUDENTS THAT ARE CROSSED OUT REPRESENT HOW MANY WILL LIKELY FAIL TO GRADUATE HIGH SCHOOL.

OUR CIRCLE, MY STORY:
HUMILITY

COPYRIGHT 2018 © TRAVIS BIGHETTY AND JASON EAGLESPEAKER

ISBN: 978-1719485609

Nekosis was excited, but scared at the same time. He was finally finishing grade 9 and would soon be leaving for the city in the fall for high school.

Nekosis wanted to become an engineer so he could help his people live better lives on the reserves. His teacher said that he was very smart and could be whatever he chose to be. While Nekosis did not listen in the morning class, when it was science and math, he was usually awake enough to pay attention to English and History.

Nekosis enjoyed the outdoors and playing hockey with his friends and cousins. Nekosis couldn't wait to get away from his pesky little sister and his overbearing mother, with all her constant hugging and kissing. Nekosis wished she wouldn't do that when his friends were close by.

Nekosis did enjoy the time with his father and being close to him whenever possible.

Nekosis' big day was finally here! Nekosis had been preparing for the past few days now. He had put away his hockey equipment, and shoved all his dirty clothes under his bed. He figured that his sister can clean up the mess when mom finds out.

Nekosis' mom managed to sneak in a family photo in his bag while he said goodbye to his friends. At the airport, his mom began to cry and hugged him for a long time. Nekosis' father did not hug his son, but simply shook his hand for the first and only time in his life. Nekosis felt like he grew a little older in that moment.

Nekosis' plane landed at the airport, and he was greeted by a strange woman. The woman said that Nekosis would be living with her while he attends school.

After a long confusing ride in the city, Nekosis arrived to his new home. The woman showed him a small room and said she would wake him up for school. There was no further conversation with the woman.

Nekosis was awoken in the morning, and told that breakfast was on the table. There were other kids in the house, but no one really talked to each other.

Nekosis sat down in the kitchen and looked at his bleak and dull breakfast. The woman told them that it was time for school. Nekosis didn't know where to go, so he followed a group of students until he came upon a large high school.

Nekosis felt lost in the large school with so many students and teachers going back and forth. He found the office and was given a schedule of his classroom, but no directions.

Nekosis tried to ask a few students where to go, but everyone was so busy. He finally found his room, but he was late for the start of class.

As he entered the classroom, Nekosis felt nervous and thought that everyone was looking at him. The teacher greeted Nekosis with a smile and asked him to find an empty seat. Nekosis sat in the back, while the teacher started going over a science lesson that made no sense to him.

The afternoon was even more confusing for Nekosis. There were different classes and teachers each time, and no one remembered Nekosis' real name.

There was one man who mentioned an after-school program where there were other Indigenous students from different communities, and that Nekosis was invited to attend.

With all the information, Nekosis forgot what was said and where to go...

Nekosis felt a little excitement when someone mentioned a hockey program. Nekosis wrote down the directions and told himself that he will find the place after school.

He went inside to find a number of kids playing hockey and having fun.

Nekosis asked a man how he can join a hockey team, or even just practice after school.

Nekosis was given a form which needed to be signed by a parent, a huge list of fees, something called a 'liability', a wavier for pictures, and a long list of restrictions.

Nekosis just wanted to skate!!

Nekosis felt like he didn't belong anywhere … not in the school, home, or at the ice rink.

The teachers didn't even say 'hi' anymore. The man from the indigenous program only stopped in for a few minutes at a time to check in. All the other indigenous students never spoke to Nekosis.

It would just seem easier to quit and disappear…

...

ABOUT THE AUTHOR

TRAVIS BIGHETTY

BORN IN THOMPSON, MANITOBA AND FROM MATHIAS COLOMB CREE NATION IN MANITOBA.

GREW UP IN NORTHERN MANITOBA AND INNER-CITY OF WINNIPEG, MANITOBA.

TRADITIONAL NAME IS MEKUNAK WHICH MEANS TURTLE. LOVE FOR COMICS AND FANTASY INFLUENCE HIS METHOD TO SHARE HIS STORY.

TRAVIS HAS WORKED WITH INDIGENOUS YOUTH AND FAMILIES FOR OVER 15 YEARS- BOYS & GIRLS CLUBS OF WINNIPEG, 7 OAKS SCHOOL DIVISION, AND OPK.

RECENTLY RECEIVED HIS MASTERS IN SOCIAL WORK.

MEMBER OF THE BEAR CLAN FOOT PATROL, COMMUNITY ADVOCATE, AND SUPER-HERO IN TRAINING.

MORE FROM EAGLESPEAKER PUBLISHING

AUTHENTICALLY INDIGENOUS NAPI STORIES:
Napi and the Rock
Napi and the Bullberries
Napi and the Wolves
Napi and the Buffalo
Napi and the Chickadees
Napi and the Coyote
Napi and the Elk
Napi and the Gophers
Napi and the Mice
Napi and the Prairie Chickens
Napi and the Bobcat
...and many more Napi tales to come

AUTHENTICALLY INDIGENOUS GRAPHIC NOVELS:
UNeducation: A Residential School Graphic Novel
Napi the Trixster: A Blackfoot Graphic Novel
UNeducation, Vol 2

AUTHENTICALLY INDIGENOUS COLORING BOOKS:
Napi: A Coloring Experience
UNeducation: A Coloring Experience
Completely Capricious Coloring Collection
A Day at the Powwow (grayscale coloring)

AUTHENTICALLY INDIGENOUS KIDS BOOKS:
Teeias Goes to a Powwow (a series)

WWW.EAGLESPEAKER.COM

**IF YOU ABSOLUTELY LOVED THIS BOOK (OR EVEN JUST KIND OF LIKED IT), PLEASE FIND IT ON AMAZON.COM AND LEAVE A QUICK REVIEW. YOUR WORDS HELP MORE THAN YOU MAY REALIZE.

Made in the USA
Columbia, SC
04 June 2018